A long life is a blessing—the elderly are living signs of the goodness of God who bestows life in abundance.

As we age, we can grow resigned to a gradual loss of energy, mobility, and mental acuity. It's easy to give in to the feeling that the best of our life is over.

We are blessed to have Pope Francis as a model of what aging can look like. Though his mobility is reduced, he still relishes the adventure of what this stage of life offers, and he finds it rich and rewarding. Far from seeing life as being "over," he preaches that there are gifts that only advanced age can offer to younger generations. In our golden years our very frailty can be a model of how to continue witnessing to the gospel in our world.

This booklet takes Pope Francis's words on aging and demonstrates what this stage of life can offer as we continue to be vibrant (if somewhat muted) members of the body of Christ. May these thirty reflections on Pope Francis's words open our eyes and hearts to how God is calling to us today.

The quotes from Pope Francis
were chosen by Deborah McCann,
who also wrote the reflections
and the "Ponder" and "Pray" pieces.

Copyright © 2023 **TWENTY-THIRD PUBLICATIONS**,
a division of Bayard; 977 Hartford Turnpike Unit A, Waterford, CT 06385;
860-437-3012 or 800-321-0411; twentythirdpublications.com.

No part of this publication may be reproduced in any manner without
prior written permission of the publisher. All rights reserved.

ISBN: 978-1-62785-784-0   ■   Printed in the U.S.A.

1 | RECOGNIZING THE CHALLENGE

Even when we are experiencing advanced age, it is hard to understand. It takes us by surprise.

No one prepares us for old age, Pope Francis says, and it can be difficult to reconcile the wrinkled and lined face we see in the mirror with the youthful person who still lives inside us. Society doesn't help, he maintains—it offers all kinds of plans for managing our health but no guides to how to live this stage of life to the full. The surprise we feel at realizing we're old is the same our young ones feel as they reach different milestones of growth. Our astonishment and acceptance can teach so much.

PONDER

What were the first signs that drew me up short and made me realize my limitations?

PRAY

God of all ages and stages, help me to accept what I cannot change and find new ways to praise you.

2 | RECOGNIZING THE GIFT

Growing old is more than the irrevocable passage of time. Aging is a blessing, not a condemnation.

If you woke up this morning, the saying goes, then you haven't finished what God has called you to do. Pope Francis echoes this sentiment to counter the feeling that we just can't keep up with the world's fast pace. "Along with old age and white hairs," he says, "God continues to give us the gift of life. If we trust in him, we will find the strength to praise him still." Illness and lack of physical strength can provide a new kind of witness for us—grace is still abundant, and we can show the young that aging is to be celebrated.

PONDER

How have I learned to cope with the changes in my body? Do I accept change gracefully or fight it?

PRAY

God of all ages and stages, let me feel strength in my weakness, so that I may bow but not be bent as I give you glory.

3 | CELEBRATING WHO WE ARE

We elderly are truly a "new people." There have never been so many of us in history.

Pope Francis praises the gift of a long life but also reminds us that with the increase in our numbers, the risk of being discarded or cast aside also grows. How can we demonstrate our vitality in the face of the culture of youth that surrounds us? Pope Francis suggests that we concentrate on what we can do that the young have less time for—like praying for others and sharing our faith journey. The serenity of old age can be a wonderful witness, as can having the time and temperament to listen.

PONDER

Have I become a better listener as I've gotten older? Have I grown in wisdom?

PRAY

God of all ages and stages, open my ears and eyes and heart to others, to show patience when impatience seems an easier response, and to share your goodness.

4 | EMBRACING A NEW RHYTHM

The arrogance of the time on the clock must be converted into the beauty of the rhythms of life.

We seniors have a new rhythm of life, Pope Francis says, one that only we can share with the young. It may not be as quick or purpose-driven as theirs, but it has its own beauty and dignity. In the face of the world's hustle and bustle, we offer a chance to stop and rest, to ponder the deeper questions of life, death, and our ultimate destination. We will spend a third of our life being old, Pope Francis stresses. It's time to hear the new music!

PONDER

What new rhythms of life have I discovered and embraced?

PRAY

God of all ages and stages, help me to respond to the newness of this stage of life. If our rhythm slows, help us to enjoy the more intricate patterns that our life lessons have given us so that our life becomes a hymn of joy.

5 | EQUAL BUT DIFFERENT

Being old is just as important and beautiful as being young. Let us remember this.

Pope Francis cautions against losing what he calls the "alliance" between generations in our "throw-away culture of productivity." We have to learn to appreciate the very different type of beauty that the elderly present—a beauty born of wisdom and experience, a beauty that reverences the slower rhythms of everyday life, a beauty that has time to share what it has learned with those who are just beginning to live their lives. This how we begin to learn to see with God's eyes.

PONDER
Do I feel diminished in my advancing years? What new gifts am I coming to recognize and accept?

PRAY
God of all ages and stages, give me your eyes to see that at this time of life I am still able to share my gifts.

6 | WHAT MATURITY REVEALS

The gift of old age is exactly that of maturity.

When he speaks of the alliance between generations, Pope Francis is encouraging us to reach out in mutual sharing with the young. More important even than advice we may have to offer is the witness our maturity bears. The very acceptance of our stage in life reflects how we continue to grow even through diminished capacity and mobility. We are uniquely positioned to demonstrate the joy of letting go, of remembering what is truly important in life.

PONDER

What have I learned about myself as I've gotten older? How gracefully do I accept the changes in my body and my mind?

PRAY

God of all ages and stages, help me to be grateful for the abilities I still possess, and help me relinquish the ones that have left me.

7 | THE BRIDGE OF WISDOM

The young must converse with the elderly, and vice versa. The bridge that results will be the transmission of wisdom in humanity.

One of the great losses of our frenetic society is the time spent just sitting and talking. Texts and social media messages, using technologies that may be difficult for some of us to follow, cannot replace the beauty of human interaction. Pope Francis is a great encourager of conversation, of the give and take that allows each generation to appreciate the experience and wisdom of the other. The bridge runs both ways, he says—we have much to share, and much still to learn.

PONDER

How good am I at listening?

PRAY

God of all ages and stages, give me the gift of patience in reaching out. Help me encourage conversation by being open to using others' ways of communicating.

8 | THE NOBILITY OF AGING

Old age shows its nobility simply by its witness.

Pope Francis is not afraid to acknowledge his own frailty in aging. Indeed, he sees moments of weakness as a spiritual gift, a chance to abandon ourselves to what God is asking of us. In this acceptance and serenity, we reveal the nobility of old age, when perhaps for the first time we are forced to see our lives through the eyes of faith—as our faculties and abilities decline, what is there left for us to do? The answer is clear. This is the time for us to *be* rather than *do*.

PONDER

Have I ever thought of my advancing years as noble? What would life look like if I did?

PRAY

God of all ages and stages, be with me as I turn my gaze ever more toward you. Help me to greet you with joy and gladness, and to use the gifts you continue to give me to demonstrate your glory.

9 | WE ARE THE ROOTS

*Let us remember that the elderly are
like the roots of a tree, and the young are
like the flowers and the fruit.*

It is helpful, Pope Francis teaches, to remember that, while we appreciate the flowers and fruit of a tree, they would not exist without a strong root system. In human terms, we are those roots, the source of our family's and culture's wisdom. We can help the following generations flower by sharing our experience, strength, and hope with them. The young can accomplish what we hope to do. Our job is to keep supplying nourishment to keep them thriving.

PONDER
How do I share my wisdom with the younger generation?

PRAY
God of all ages and stages, let me look to you as the bedrock of any wisdom I possess, and help me to share this with others.

10 | DIALOGUE: A HUMAN NEED

*A young person who is not bonded to
his or her grandparents does not grow up well.
Without the roots that grandparents provide,
a child grows up without points of reference.*

Dialogue between generations is essential, Pope Francis says, in order for the continuity of human life to be maintained. And it helps to skip a generation here. Parents are busy with the day-to-day duties of bringing up their children. Grandparents have more time to engage on deeper levels of imagination and wisdom. The elderly truly have an irreplaceable opportunity to guide the lives of the younger generation. Grandparents form the root system that allows generations to flourish.

PONDER

Do I communicate better with my grandchildren than with my own children?

PRAY

God of all ages and stages, help me to frame the wisdom of age with the innocence of youth.

11 | A BEAUTIFUL SYMPHONY

May God help us find the right music for this harmonious relationship among the various ages—everyone together: the little ones, the elderly, adults.

Pope Francis uses the image of music to paint a picture of the glorious symphony that can exist when all generations are in tune with one another. Children wonder and imagine, adults need to seek advice and counsel, and the elderly have the life experience of trial and error to be present to all. It is for this reason, the pope maintains, that no part of the generational fabric is unimportant or insignificant. We all need to learn from one another and add the richness of our voices to the communal song.

PONDER

How can I improve my dialogue with my children and grandchildren? Which part of the symphony is mine to contribute?

PRAY

God of all ages and stages, teach me my part in your great symphony of love.

12 | PASSING HISTORY ALONG

An old age that is granted the clarity of seeing history and passing it on is a precious gift for the next generation. Being able to listen personally and directly to the story of lived faith, with all its highs and lows, is irreplaceable.

Pope Francis stresses that it is the mission of the elderly to pass along the stories of the past that have helped make us who we are today. And stories of faith should be an integral part of this sharing. Faith, Pope Francis emphasizes, is caught, not taught. While parents may be busy in the act of getting children ready for church and faith formation, grandparents can share what the faith means and how it has played a significant role in daily life.

PONDER

How can my lived faith experience point the way for my grandchildren?

PRAY

God of all ages and stages, help me find the words to make you come alive for others.

13 | A NEW SPIRITUAL JOURNEY

One gift of being elderly is learning to abandon oneself to the care of others. This starts by abandoning ourselves to God himself.

Old age, they say, is not for sissies. Pope Francis acknowledges this frequently, but he also reminds us that this is yet another way that God is reaching out to us. As our years increase, we need to rely more on having others care for us, a hard thing for many of us to accept, especially when it means no longer living on our own, having to live by others' schedules, and the like. But within this is the gift of beginning to find God in every minute. Each new adjustment can reveal where and how God is acting in our lives. What great wisdom to share with others!

PONDER
What new strengths have I gained as other abilities have diminished?

PRAY
God of all ages and stages, show me how to trust you and abandon myself to your will.

14 | A DAZZLING WITNESS

When the elderly person who is open speaks to a young person who is open, he or she bids farewell to life while "handing over" life to the new generation.

So much of growing old involves letting go—as we elderly are stripped down to our essence, what remains is the solid core of faith. Children are hungry for this, and there's no one better than we are to pass this along. The faith we hand on can become the bedrock of the next generation's experience of God, to shore them up when life throws its inevitable curves. Our infirmity is, as Pope Francis says, a "dazzling witness" of faith and trust in the God who loves us.

PONDER

Has my faith grown over the years? What part of my faith journey would speak to others?

PRAY

God of all ages and stages, let my witness of faith be as positive as your love for me.

15 | A REVOLUTION OF TENDERNESS

Old age is no time to give up and lower the sails. It is a time of enduring fruitfulness: a new mission awaits us and bids us look to the future.

Pope Francis calls for us to stage a "nonviolent revolution" of tenderness at this time of our life. As the current matriarchs and patriarchs of our families, we are called to *love* harder and more fiercely than ever. This is our chance to cherish and accept the gifts God has given us, especially our children and their children, and even further down the line. When we show our love for the generations that will succeed us, we are demonstrating our faith in God's good work in us, through us, and for us.

PONDER
Do I make opportunities to tell my loved ones how much they are loved?

PRAY
God of all ages and stages, give me the strength to love with your fidelity and compassion.

16 | OUR LOVING GAZE

*We have grown in humanity by caring for others.
Now we can be teachers of a way of life that is peaceful
and attentive to those in greatest need.*

To love others, Pope Francis reminds us, is a decision, one that we need to make every day. It's something we have learned, for better or worse, over the years. At this stage of our lives, we need to become ever more mindful of what is important—teaching others to be understanding and caring in our place. This is all part of the letting go that Pope Francis calls us to do with a cheerful, confident, faith-filled spirit. When we pass on a tradition of loving, we are sharing the greatest gift there is.

PONDER

Do I make the decision to love others each day? Has this gotten easier through the years?

PRAY

God of all ages and stages, open my heart in loving acceptance of others, and help me to teach others how to love as you do.

17 | OUR NEW VOCATION

*Our vocation today is to preserve our roots,
to pass on the faith to the young,
and to care for the little ones.*

Our task of passing on history, faith, and love to the coming generations is more than a duty, Pope Francis says. It is a true vocation. When we look at it through this lens, it becomes holy work, challenging and rewarding in equal measure. We engage in the imaginative world of the little ones. We may also, by our graceful acceptance or decreased ability, show the next generation that old age is not to be feared, airbrushed away, or ignored. We have a real chance to witness the beauty of advancing years. Let us embrace it with full hearts.

PONDER
How truly accepting am I of this new stage of life?

PRAY
God of all ages and stages, help me to embrace each new challenge with joy so that I may give you praise.

18 | THE THREE PILLARS

Dreams, memory, and prayer: God will grant us all, even the frailest among us, the strength we need to embark on this new journey.

Pope Francis gives us the hallmarks we need to make the most of our new vocation. Dreams, memory, and prayer are the tools that will help us build "the world of tomorrow" in "fraternity and social friendship." This is a task of contemplation in action—to share the longings of our hearts, the events that have made us who we are, and the faith that has guided us in our path. We are uniquely equipped, the pope says, to offer these gifts to the world.

PONDER
Am I ready to begin my new vocation?

PRAY
God of all ages and stages, help me to use the events of my life—tangible gifts as well as blessings in disguise—in your service, as I seek to do your will to create a new and better world for the generations to come.

19 | THE DREAMS OF THE PRESENT: THE HOPE OF THE FUTURE

The young can take the dreams of the elderly and make them come true. Yet for this to happen, we must continue to dream.

Pope Francis reminds us that the young are the ones to put our dreams into action. As the saying goes, it is a sign of true faith to plant a tree whose shade you'll never see. When we share our dreams with the young, we are demonstrating our confidence in them and in God, who makes all things possible. What an extraordinary gift to share!

PONDER

How can I express the dreams I have for the future so that the young will be inspired?

PRAY

God of all ages and stages, please grant me the ability to paint my dreams in vivid colors so that the young will be able to make them a reality in the times to come.

20 | MEMORY: THE FOUNDATION OF LIFE

A true mission for every elderly person is keeping memory alive and sharing it with others.

Without a solid foundation, Pope Francis says, we cannot build a house. And memory is that solid foundation in our lives. It gives shape and focus to our dreams for the future. The pope especially calls on us elderly who have the experience and memory of war to share that with our young people, so that they can work toward eliminating that horror from their lives and the lives of their children. If we hope for a better future, we must not shrink from confronting the legacy of the past.

PONDER

Are there parts of the past that I hesitate to share? Am I protecting myself or hindering positive change?

PRAY

God of all ages and stages, help me to use my memories to build a better world.

21 | PRAYER: THE MOST IMPORTANT PILLAR

Prayer is the deep breath that both the world and the Church urgently need.

Admittedly, it's hard to adjust to the loss of physical stamina as we age. Pope Francis frequently speaks of this, saying how much he relies on prayer as an active practice. It isn't the only thing we can do as our physical ability declines, he says, but it is the most important thing, a practice that maintains focus and balance in our often troubled world. To practice this kind of active contemplation is a gift that we are uniquely positioned to share with the world.

PONDER
Do I find myself praying more these days? Do I accept prayer as a gift I can offer to the Church?

PRAY
God of all ages and stages, help me to realize that there are always new ways for me to contribute to your unending dialogue with all your children.

22 | RESTORING FAITH'S HONOR

We aren't new at this anymore. How we witness the faith may change, but it is no less steadfast.

"The practice of faith is not the symbol of our weakness," Pope Francis says, "but rather the sign of its strength." As always, he is not speaking in the abstract, but very much from his own experience of a person growing older and needing to find new ways of being useful in and to the world. He speaks, too, of our responsibility of restoring the honor of the faith—this is hardly a retreat into inactivity. Instead, it is a call to new and vibrant action as witnesses of what God is continuing to do with, in, and through us.

PONDER

How am I adjusting to a life that is both more sedentary and yet more active? Is my prayer life improving?

PRAY

God of all ages and stages, keep me hopeful each and every day so that others will see you in me.

23 | HUMANIZING THE FUTURE

By being with their grandparents, little ones learn the power of tenderness and respect for frailty.

When we spend time with our grandchildren, we aren't just helping them, Pope Francis says. We are helping our children too, because the little ones will learn how to care for people who can't run as fast, or as long, who need to take time just to catch their breath, whose idea of play is to spin imaginative tales or gently guide them in the faith. By spending time with us, they will learn to be kinder and more attentive to their parents as they age. This is a crucial lesson that no other age can teach. We are an integral part of this growth.

PONDER

Do I feel bad when I can't keep up with my grandchildren, or do I see my frailty as a way to teach kindness?

PRAY

God of all ages and stages, help me to enjoy each and every moment that brings me closer to you.

24 | LET THE WORLD PAY HEED

God has given talents to everyone, made to fit each person, including the elderly. Our communities must learn how to benefit from their talents and charisms.

"A wealth to be treasured" is how Pope Francis refers to us elderly. The gifts God shares with us now are the gifts of patient listening, learning, teaching, advising—in every way paying attention to the needs of others. The wisdom and experience we have gleaned over our lifetime is now to be given away. We know how to look and how to see, Pope Francis tells us—that is perhaps the greatest gift we can share. There is still so much left for us to do. Let us keep reminding the world that we're still here.

PONDER

What has been my greatest strength in life?
What is it now?

PRAY

God of all ages and stages, help me to be open to developing new skills, so that I can still make a difference in the world.

25 | THE BEAUTY OF AGING

Old age is not an obstacle to the being born anew that Jesus speaks of. It becomes the perfect time to illuminate it.

Don't hide wrinkles or frailty, Pope Francis urges us. They are the signs of a life lived with all its joys and sorrows. We were first born anew in our baptism. Now, old age is pointing us toward that closer embrace with God—of life eternal. Our witness of this is so important for the generations to come. A life lived with the serene confidence of faith is a beautiful thing to see. And our stooped shoulders and wrinkled faces only give credence to our continued trust that God will use us well.

PONDER

Do I accept the face I see in the mirror? Do I accept that God loves me just as I am?

PRAY

God of all ages and stages, I thank you for the blessing of a long life well lived. May I always give you praise.

26 | THIS IS WHAT GOD IS LIKE

The tenderness of the elderly opens the door to understanding God's tenderness.

One thing we can always do, no matter how old or frail we become, is *love*. And Pope Francis says that all we need to do is look at how grandparents gaze at their grandchildren to begin to understand the immense unconditional love of God. That tenderness, he continues, is a true reflection of God's unending care for us. As we build that intergenerational bridge, our own children can begin to see how much we have loved them as well. Who could have foreseen that at this stage of life we would so clearly manifest the face of God?

PONDER
How much or how little am I revealing God's love in the world?

PRAY
God of all ages and stages, free me from whatever keeps me from reflecting your face to everyone I meet.

27 | THE PURITY OF GRATITUDE

If the elderly were placed at the center of collective attention, instead of being rejected and dismissed, they would be encouraged to exercise the valuable ministry of gratitude toward God, who forgets no one.

Pope Francis is very sensitive to the illnesses that become more numerous and more serious as we age, and how society often reacts to this by shunting the elderly to one side. Far from this bleak scenario, the pope says, we elderly have a chance not only to demonstrate God's love but also to express what he calls the "ministry of gratitude"—gratitude for our long life, gratitude for the ability still to praise and give God glory.

PONDER
How has my view of aging changed as I have gotten older and frailer?

PRAY
God of all ages and stages, let everything I do be a sign of your goodness.

28 | GOOD WINE ONCE AGED

*We women and men of a certain age
have the possibility of wisdom. We still have
glad tidings to share.*

Above all, Pope Francis stresses, we who have reached this stage of life must not give in to the "grim resignation" that society would impose on us. Filled with the gifts of pure love, joyful gratitude, and well-earned wisdom, we have so much to offer the world. This does run counter to what much of society tells us is our role—being unseen and unheard. Rather, we are called to herald the future by reminding the next generations of what is truly important.

PONDER

What one gift can I still share with others that is unique to me?

PRAY

God of all ages and stages, help me to keep my voice when others say I have nothing left to contribute. Let my wisdom speak.

29 | THE PRESENT AND THE PROMISE

The witness of the elderly brings together the ages of life and the very dimensions of time, for they are not only the memory; they are the present as well as the promise.

By living vibrantly in the present and guiding future generations to find their footing, we elderly represent the best of what has been. By being bridge builders, we both forge the way and offer guidance along the path. Pope Francis says that we "unite the ages of time," a wonderful image of the significance of our witness. This is an achievement to be celebrated!

PONDER

Do I feel that I am still an important part of the life around me?

PRAY

God of all ages and stages, guide my steps as I offer my counsel to my children and grandchildren, and on through the ages.

30 | THE BEST IS YET TO COME

*Old age, lived in the expectation of the Lord,
can become a testament of faith,
which reveals our hope for all.*

Far from "waiting to die," Pope Francis looks on aging and the gift of old age as waiting to *live*. This means using our time to sow seeds of goodness, kindness, tenderness, and wisdom wherever and however we can. He himself is a witness to this—as his frailties increase, he shares them with us so that we can embrace our own. He is unafraid of the future because he knows that God will use us, however we are able, to give God glory. There is no greater gift!

PONDER

How am I witnessing to God's goodness today?

PRAY

God of all ages and stages, help me to push past fear, hold on to hope, and use every ache and pain, and every moment of joy or sadness, to praise you!